Rookie
Talk About It™

Optimism:
Sunny-Side Up!

by Jodie Shepherd

Content Consultant
Samantha Gambino, Psy.D.
Licensed Psychologist, New York, New York

Reading Consultant
Jeanne M. Clidas, Ph.D.
Reading Specialist

Children's Press®
An Imprint of Scholastic Inc.

A CIP catalog record of this book is available from the Library of Congress.
ISBN 978-0-531-21515-9 (library binding) – ISBN 978-0-531-21383-4 (pbk.)

Produced by Spooky Cheetah Press
Design by Keith Plechaty

All rights reserved. Published in 2016 by Children's Press, an imprint of Scholastic Inc.

Printed in China 62

SCHOLASTIC, CHILDREN'S PRESS, ROOKIE TALK ABOUT IT™, and associated logos are trademarks and/or registered trademarks of Scholastic Inc.

1 2 3 4 5 6 7 8 9 10 R 25 24 23 22 21 20 19 18 17 16

Photographs ©: cover: Edith Held/Corbis Images; 3 top left: Denis Kovin/Shutterstock, Inc.; 3 top right: snake3d/Shutterstock, Inc.; 3 bottom: Vitalinka/Shutterstock, Inc.; 4: Inara Prusakova/Shutterstock, Inc.; 7: Rommel/Masterfile; 8: Jupiterimages/Thinkstock; 11: Evgeni_S/Shutterstock, Inc.; 12: Antonio_Diaz/Thinkstock; 15: ColorBlind Images/Media Bakery; 16: karens4/Thinkstock; 19: Marjorie Kamys Cotera/Daemmrich Photos/The Image Works; 20: Peter Cade/Getty Images; 23: imageBroker/Alamy Images; 24: Jarenwicklund/Dreamstime; 26: Bettmann/Corbis Images; 27: Mary Evans Picture Library/Alamy Images; 28: Nanette Grebe/Shutterstock, Inc.; 29: Mike Kemp/Media Bakery; 30: KidStock/Media Bakery; 31 top: Chris Hendrickson/Masterfile/Corbis Images; 31 center top: airdone/Thinkstock; 31 center bottom: Nanette Grebe/Shutterstock, Inc.; 31 bottom: Peter Cade/Getty Images.

Table of Contents

What Is Optimism?

Imagine you walk outside one morning. It is a sunny day, but there are clouds in the sky, too. So what do you see? Is it partly cloudy? Or is it partly sunny? An **optimist** would say, "Partly sunny," for sure!

"Look on the sunny side." Have you ever heard anyone say that? It means you should focus on the good things in life instead of the bad.

Optimism is the belief that good things are going to happen. It does not mean there will not be difficulties. It does not mean things will always be easy. But it is a way of looking at the world and thinking that things will work out.

Being Grateful

Look around you. Do you have people who care about you? Do you have a friend? It is important to notice all the good things in your life. If you want to be an optimistic person, feeling **gratitude** is a good place to start.

Everything in life has good things *and* bad things about it. A rose is a beautiful flower, but it has sharp thorns. An optimist focuses on the good things. That is called positive thinking. It feels better!

The following pages have stories about kids who are being postive. Read their stories and think about how you would feel in their place.

thorn

Positive Thinkers

Playing the guitar is not easy for Emma. She has friends who play better than she does. That makes her upset sometimes. But she knows that the more she practices, the better she will play. Besides, Emma plays the guitar because she enjoys it. Optimistic people enjoy what they do.

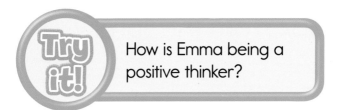

Try it! How is Emma being a positive thinker?

Lucas is telling his dad about what a great day he had. Nothing big or special happened. But lots of little nice things did. Even some not-so-great things happened!

But Lucas remembers all the things that made him happy. He shared cookies with his mom after school. He played kickball with his friends at recess. And he picked a great new book from the library.

Every evening, write down one thing that went well that day, or one thing that you felt grateful for. Before long, you will feel better about life.

Jayden and Chloe are working on a puzzle together. Jayden is feeling **frustrated**. There is one piece that they just cannot find. "Don't worry," says Chloe. "I know we will figure it out if we just keep trying!"

How is Chloe being optimistic?

Steven has been having trouble with math. Sometimes, doing homework gets him really frustrated. On those nights, he just wants to give up!

Instead, Steven asks his dad for help. And he studies hard every day. He knows deep down that he will succeed. That is what gives him the strength to **persevere**.

Gabriel has been trying to climb the rope in gym for weeks. But he just cannot reach the top! At the end of class, he feels angry and disappointed in himself.

Then Gabriel reminds himself to think positive. Tomorrow is another day—and another chance to try again.

Jessie is learning to skate. She falls a lot. At the end of her lesson, she often feels cold, sore, and cranky! She does not think she will ever get the hang of this.

After a while, though, Jessie tries to look on the bright side. She thinks, "Every day I am getting one step closer to learning how to skate."

Are you optimistic, like the kids in these stories? Do you look on the sunny side of life? If so, you will find that a good attitude can make even bad things seem better.

Share your optimism. Greet your friends and family with a friendly "hi" and a smile. You will probably get the same in return.

Helen Keller

Helen Keller was born in Alabama in 1880. By the time she was two years old, a very serious childhood illness had left her completely unable to see, hear, and talk. She was cut off from everyone and everything around her. Then teacher Anne Sullivan taught her a way of communicating by sign language. Since Helen could not see, Anne used her fingers to spell and sign right into Helen's hand. From then on, Helen never stopped learning.

Helen became a writer and lecturer. She helped millions of people all around the world who had disabilities and other challenges. She inspired them to find happiness in their lives. In her book *Optimism*, Helen wrote "Optimism is the faith that leads to achievement. Nothing can be done without hope and confidence."

Here are some ways to practice being optimistic even when it is hard to do:

1. Smile. When you smile often, you can put yourself in a good mood.

2. Be grateful for what you have.

3. Celebrate your strengths.

4. Spend your time thinking about the good things that happen. Do not focus on the bad things.

Read the story below and imagine what you might do in this situation.

You are supposed to have a baseball game today. You have been looking forward to it all week. But when you wake up, it is cold and rainy. What should you do?

Need help getting started?

- How might you look on the bright side? Are there fun things you can do indoors?

- How can you keep a positive attitude? What might you say to keep others from feeling down?

Are You an Optimist?

1. When your dad buys you an ice-cream cone, what do you think?

   a. What a yummy treat!

   b. Too bad there are no sprinkles on top.

2. When you do not do well on a test, how do you feel?

   a. Next time I will be more prepared.

   b. Boy, I blew that!

3. When you come in second in a race, what do you think?

   a. I keep getting better; I was really close this time.

   b. I lost; I am not going to do this again.

If you answered mostly with As, you are an optimist! If you chose mostly Bs, you should try to look on the sunny side more often!

Glossary

frustrated (FRUHSS-trayt-ed): feeling helpless or discouraged

gratitude (GRAT-uh-tood) feeling of being thankful and grateful for things

optimist (OP-tuh-mist): person who believes things will work out for the best

persevere (pur-suh-VEER): keep working at something until you finish

Index

Facts for Now

Visit this Scholastic Web site for more information on optimism:
www.factsfornow.scholastic.com
Enter the keyword **Optimism**

About the Author

Jodie Shepherd, who also writes under the name Leslie Kimmelman, is an award-winning author of dozens of books for children, both fiction and nonfiction. She is a children's book editor, too.